IMAGINE

A CELEBRATION OF
JOHN LENNON

PENGUIN
STUDIO

Imagine there's no heaven

It's easy if you try

NO
HELL
BELOW
US

NO
HELL
BELOW
US

Above us
only sky

Imagine all the people

Living for today

IMAGINE
THERE'S NO COUNTRY

It isn't hard to do

NOTHING
TO KILL OR
DIE FOR

NOTHING
TO KILL OR
DIE FOR

And no religion too

Imagine all the people
Living life in peace

You may say
I'm a dreamer

But I'm not the only one

I hope someday

you'll join us

And the world
will be one

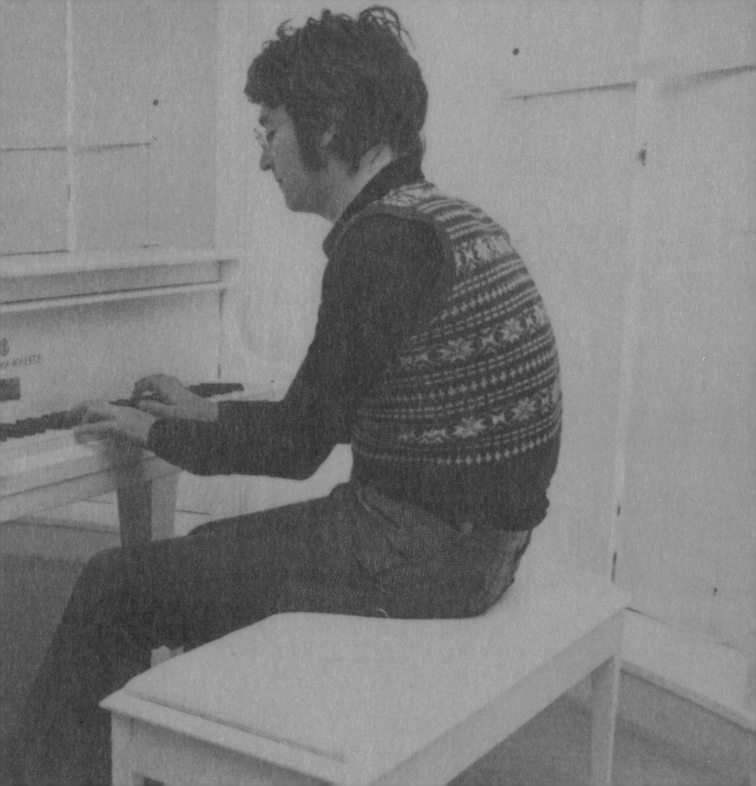

Imagine no possessions

I wonder if you can

NO NEED FOR GREED OR HUNGER

A brotherhood of man

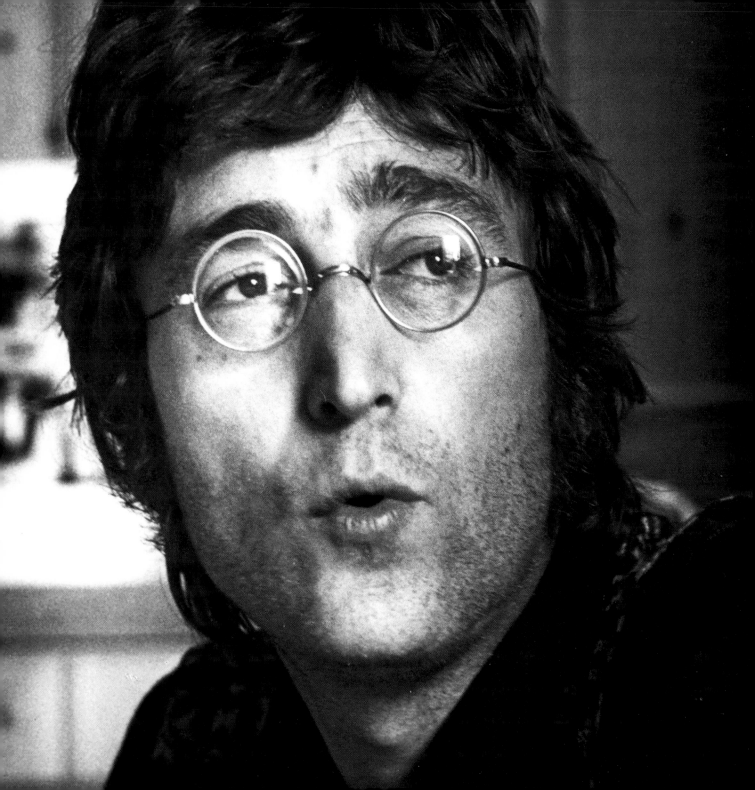

Imagine
all the people
sharing all
the world

Imagine
all the people
sharing all
the world

You may say I'm a dreamer

But I'm not the only one

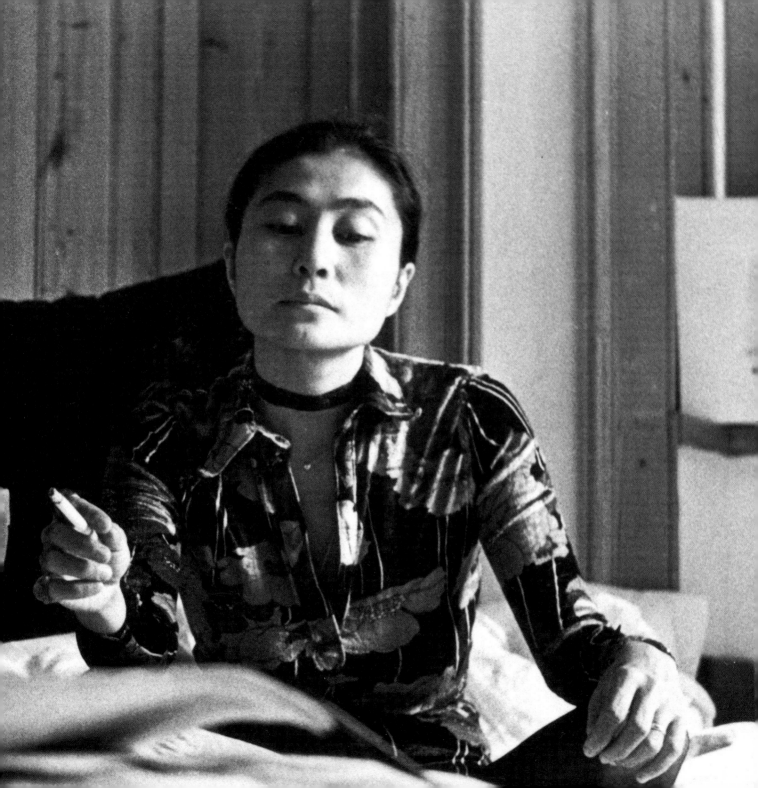

I hope someday
you'll join us

AND
THE
WORLD
WILL
LIVE
AS
ONE

Acknowledgments

The publishers wish to thank the following copyright holders
for their permission to reproduce illustrations supplied:

Tom Hanley: Cover, Pages 4-5, 7, 11-13, 15, 18-19, 23, 25, 28, 30, 32-33, 36-37 and 41-43.
Tom Hanley's pictures of John and Yoko were taken in August 1971 at Tittenhurst Park, Ascot, where they had lived for about two years.
During a long and intimate photo session John played, at the white piano, all the songs he and Paul McCartney had written together;
then he played *'Imagine'*, which he had just completed. Tom, providentially, was one of the first people to hear the song.

Redferns: Pages 8, 22, 26, and 31. • Starfile: Pages 9, 16, 21, and 35. • Range/Bettemann/UPI: Pages 14, 27 and 29.
Retna Pictures: Pages 34 and 39. • Sioux Nesi: The Albert Watson Studio: Page 44.

PENGUIN STUDIO

Published by the Penguin Group
Penguin Books USA Inc., 375 Hudson Street, New York, New York 10014, U.S.A.
Penguin Books Ltd, 27 Wrights Lane, London W8 5TZ, England
Penguin Books Australia Ltd, Ringwood, Victoria, Australia
Penguin Books Canada Ltd, 10 Alcorn Avenue, Toronto, Ontario, Canada M4V 3B2
Penguin Books (N.Z.) Ltd, 182-190 Wairau Road, Auckland 10, New Zealand

Penguin Books Ltd, Registered Offices: Harmondsworth, Middlesex, England

First American edition
Published in 1996 by Viking Penguin, a division of Penguin Books USA Inc.

10 9 8 7 6 5 4 3 2 1   1 3 5 7 9 10 8 6 4 2   1 2 3 4 5 6 7 8 9 10

'Imagine'
Words and Music by John Lennon.
Copyright © 1971 Lenono Music for the World.
Used by permission. All Rights Reserved.

ISBN 0-670-86690-3

Designed by Wherefore Art?
Additional photography by Dan Einzig

Printed and bound in Singapore by Tien Wah Press